Table Of Contents

Foreword

Chapter 1:
Introduction

Chapter 2:
Why Build A List

Chapter 3:
Basics Of List Building

Chapter 4:
Traffic Building

Chapter 5:
Ad Swaps

Chapter 6:
Giveaway Events

Chapter 7:
Speedlist Building

Chapter 8:
List Building Mistakes

Wrapping Up

Foreword

Do you have an email list? How big is your list?

List building is an integral part of any online business. Just as how brick and mortar businesses keep record of their previous customers, the online entrepreneur has to collect the information of his visitors so that he can contact them again later on.

Therefore, huge focus must be placed on learning how to build a powerful mailing list so that you can continuously provide value to your prospects or customers at the same time monetize from them.

Are you ready to build a highly profitable list in your online business? Let's get started.

List Landslide

Build Your List The Fast Way Using Powerful Free And Paid Methods

Chapter 1:

Introduction

Synopsis

The money is in the list, they say.

Intro

What is a list, exactly? Basically, it's short for **email marketing list** or **email autoresponder list**. These emails are the contact information of visitors who come to your site who are looking for specific information on your niche topic.

In order to build a list, you will need to have an email autoresponder set up. The two most common autoresponders in the market are:

-Get response (www.getresponse.com)
-Aweber (www.aweber.com)

It is **compulsory** for anyone who wishes to start an online business to get an autoresponder account. This will be used to manage your subscribers and mass email your list with offers and information of interest.

Fortunately, these autoresponders come in different packages for big and small entrepreneurs, so choose your desired package wisely.

Once you have an autoresponder account set up, you'll have to set up a business system for collecting leads or subscribers, which I will detail in chapter 3: The basics of list building.

Chapter 2:
Why Build A List?

Synopsis

One of the most common question asked by new online marketers is: **"Do I Have To Build A List?"**

Do You Need It

The truth is, there are many ways to make money online. Some make money through blogging, which involves getting readers hooked onto your blog content and wanting to come back everyday to read new stuff. While others dabble with e-commerce or drop-shipping.

However, if you are in the business of information marketing, it is highly recommended that you build an email list.

Why is that?

With an email list, not only can you continuously build rapport with your subscribers, you can also offer them products of interest. Traffic that comes and is not captured is a waste. People are looking for specific information and they will leave forever once they have found out. However, if you manage to capture their emails, you can continue to provide value and turn them into your loyal customers or followers.

One more good reason – With an email autoresponder, you can automate emails so that new subscribers will automatically be funneled through a series of emails which will lead to a sale eventually. Can you say *passive income*?

Chapter 3:
Basics Of List Building

Synopsis

So how do you start building a list, exactly?

How Do You Do It

You will first need to set up your list funnel. It typically consists of 3 components:

1) Landing page or Squeeze Page
2) Free Gift or "Bribe"
3) Opt in box

The landing page is a simple one page website which consists of a headline, sub headline, pitch & benefits and call to action.

The headline has to be eye-catching and bolded to immediately get your reader's attention. The sub headline will reinforce the message of the headline.

The purpose of the page is to "bribe" a visitor to enter his name and email in exchange for a free gift. This could be an e-book, e-course or weekly newsletter.

The benefits are meant to explain what the reader would get from this free gift and to improve sign up rates.

Finally, in the call to action, you inform the reader that they must enter their name and email to get the free gift.

The place where the reader enters his contact information is known as the "opt in box", which can be obtained from to email autoresponder host website. Autoresponders like Getresponse offer easy customizations for opt-in boxes to make boxes suit your site layout easier.

Alternatively, you can choose to put your opt in box in your blog or website to collect subscribers. The choice is entirely yours but landing pages often have higher opt in rates because visitors only have less choices – Opt in or don't as compared to blogs.

Voila! **You've just set up your list building system!**

Chapter 4:
Traffic Building

Synopsis

Now that you've set up for list building funnel, the next important part of building a huge email list is traffic generation.

Traffic

You see, list building is pretty much a math game. The more people you send to your website or landing page, the more probability someone would opt into your list to get your free gift.

Now that we've agreed on that, let's have a look at some nifty traffic generation techniques ☺

First up we have article submission. This is the bread and butter of drawing traffic. By submitting articles to article directories such as EzineArticles (www.ezinearticles.com) and GoArticles (www.goarticles.com), you can draw a steady stream of readers into your website.

You can also consider starting a blog to gain readership. Post articles of value related to your niche and at the end of blog posts, link to your landing page, offering them a free gift as a kind gesture for following your blog. If you are good at SEO, you can draw massive organic search traffic to your blog or landing page as well.

Google advertising is difficult for landing pages, and it won't get approved easily. Here's a better way – use Facebook advertising to get followers to "Like" your fan page. The fan page can serve as a platform for your followers to interact and from there the possibilities are endless. You can either send them to your opt in page or put an opt in box on your fan page if you are web programming savvy.

Here's another way to draw traffic fast. Post interesting YouTube videos on topics related to your niche. Make it as interesting as possible for it to go viral.

In the description of your videos, provide a brief description and include a link to your landing page to download a free gift such as an e-book. That way, you can leverage on the power of word of mouth to reach out to a wider target audience.

The key is, pick one traffic generation technique, get good at it and move on to the next one. That way, in no time you'll be swimming in a sea of subscribers!

Chapter 5:
Ad Swaps

Synopsis

Ad swaps is by far one of the fastest ways to build your list fast. Basically, it involves exchanging promo emails between 2 different marketers of a similar niche.

Ads

Remember, the two people doing the ad swap must be in a similar niche for it to be effective. List size and quality is also very important so make sure you know you swap partner well.

There are also several ad swapping membership sites where you can find many like minded people to exchange lists with each other such as SafeSwaps (www.safe-swaps.com).

You might have to pay a monthly fee for it but since you'll be able to build a huge list through swaps its quite worth it.

Here's a few tips for an effective ad swap:

-Try to find out more about your swap partner's business. Understanding his niche and his teachings will help give you a better idea as to whether his products will improve the quality of your list or degrade it.

-If possible, get your partner to verify his list size and do the same for him. Trust is an important factor in successful networking. Once you've broken the barriers between both parties there will be more room for future collaboration.

-Keep the fire burning. After a successful swap, find other ways for collaboration such as doing JV launches or promoting each other's paid products.

Remember, when used correctly, ad swaps can help you achieve much more in less time!

Chapter 6:
Giveaway Events

Synopsis

Giveaway events are great places to build your list fast. A giveaway event is a place where various contributors will contribute a free gift such as an e-book or video course and people who are looking for these goodies can come and get them for free, all they have to do is opt in to the respective lists.

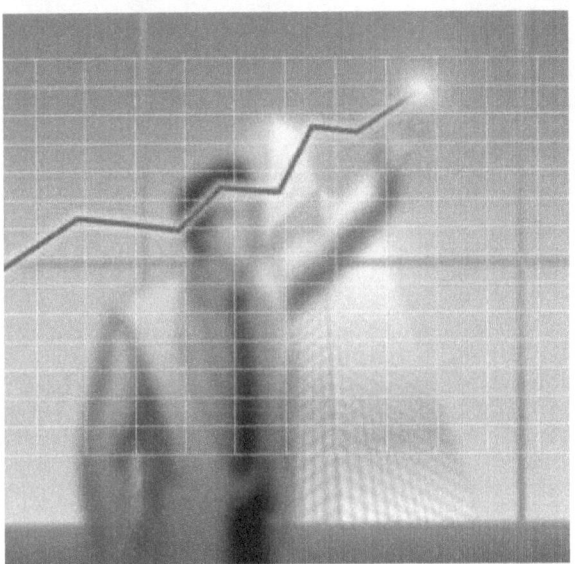

Giveaways

You can either choose to be a contributor or you can be the organizer. If you wish to be a contributor, you will have to contribute a gift and promote the launch to your list in order to get a better ad space for your free gift. The more people you refer to the giveaway, the more eyeballs your free gift will get and hence more opt ins.

If you choose to be the organizer, you will have to invite contributors and coordinate the whole event launch. You will have to set up the giveaway website either by purchasing a giveaway manager program or create the website yourself.

One of the common giveaway managers used is Giveaway Manager 2 (www.giveawaymanager2.com)

In short, a giveaway event can not only help you generate a big list fast, but can also help you network and connect with other like minded marketers for future joint venture opportunities.

Chapter 7:
Speed List Building

Synopsis

Do you want to build your list at lightning speed?

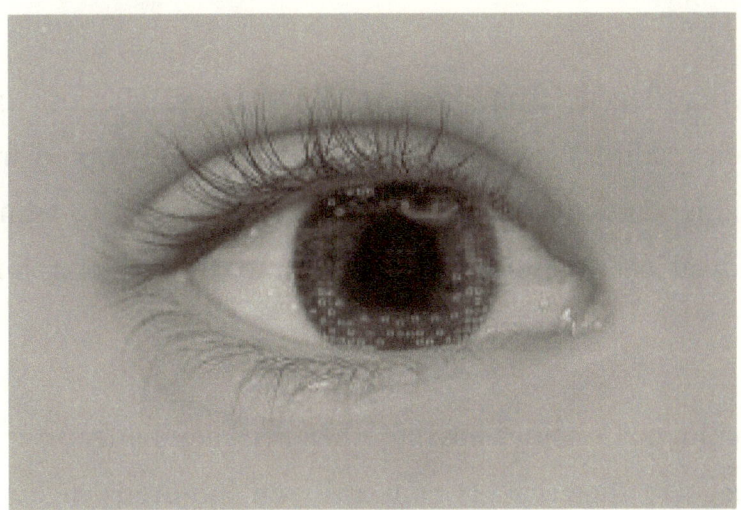

How To

If you are on a shoestring budget, organically building your list from free traffic methods are the way to go.

However, if you have some spare cash or have set a marketing budget for yourself, consider speeding up your list building process by leveraging on systems, which will help you grow it faster.

That is the only way you can truly bring your business to the next level. Here's a few great ideas for speeding up your list building process.

-Consider buying leads from reputable sources. Places like GetResponse sell qualified leads which are automatically opted into your autoresponder and if you have a good email series to funnel them through, you can definitely turn them into your long term customers.

-Pay for solo mailings. Consider paying other marketers a fee to mail your landing page to their list. It can save you hundreds of hours trying to get subscribers the normal way.

-Outsource traffic generation. Higher ghostwriters to blog for you and draw traffic to your landing page. This option can be cheaper than you think.

-Adopt the 80/20 principle. Also known as the Pareto's Principle, it states that 80% of our results spur from 20% of our efforts and 20% of our results from 80% of the effort. Thus, identify which 20% of the effort is helping you grow your list fast and put in more steam into that. Eliminate the useless stuff!

Remember, if you think big, so will the size of your list be. If you think small, the same goes for your list size.

Chapter 8:
List Building Mistakes

Synopsis

This special Chapter is about helping you avoid the pitfalls that marketers make when building their list. Every marketer who has started list building has made such mistakes, and with this chapter, you will not have to make the same errors as they have so you can speed up your list building process!

Mistakes

Mistake #1 – Buying leads before setting up a proper autoresponder email series.

If you put the horse before the cart, you will end up leaving tons of money on the table because you won't be able to convert your fresh leads into hungry customers – Your leads will turn cold.

Mistake #2 – Giving up too fast.

Rome wasn't built in a day, and the same goes for list building. You'll have to put in conscious effort and put your efforts in diligently if you want to see leads pouring into your funnel. For example, some blogs or website may even take months before they appear on Google or have a good Page rank.

Mistake #3 – Spamming your leads with useless rubbish.

Each time you promote something, make sure that offer is something that will truly benefit your customers.

You lose karma points each time you promote something so make it count. Make sure you achieve a balance of providing useful free content and self promotion.

Mistake #4 – Making too many ad swaps.

Ad swaps might be a good way to build your list, but you must remember each time that you promote another person's product; you are literally *giving away* your potential customers to your competitors. This can draw their attention away from the value you have to offer and thus the quality of your list may suffer.

In short, do your best to avoid these mistakes and always adopt good list building practices to ensure maximal quality and quantity of subscribers.

Wrapping Up

The ability of your list to make money is not just determined by size, but also by the quality of your subscribers. It is therefore important that you nurture and treat your list well.

Rome wasn't built in a day, the same way having a huge list doesn't happen in an instant. However, if you diligently practice these list building methods, it is 100% that you will be bringing in streams of hot subscribers into your email list.

The best way for success in list building is by eliminating what fails to work and trying new stuff to see what really works.

Once you have found what works best for your business, replicate and multiply your efforts and in no time, you've built yourself a solid business empire streaming with thousands of followers.

I wish you all the best in your list building endeavors!

www.ingramcontent.com/pod-product-compliance
Lightning Source LLC
Chambersburg PA
CBHW030603220526
45463CB00007B/3157